Inconsolable

Inconsolable

By Roberto Carlos Martinez

Edited by Rosario Garcia

PandaMonk
PUBLISHING

ISBN-13: 978-0990517610
ISBN-10: 0990517616
PandaMonk Publishing, LLC
Alexandria, Virginia

For my father,

Roberto Martinez.

Everything is not forgotten.

You've done the best from your point of view

but still there's more to tell.

Table of Contents

Third Eye

INCONSOLABLE

Poor

Somewhere along the tracks,
the whistling and the echoes,
those who believed stopped believing,
lost in their perfection,
in the meaning of the words,
in the lies they told themselves and each other.

Somewhere along the tracks the lights
changed colors.
Dreams became more aggressive,
realities more like dreams.

Fly Backwards

Hummingbird,
sweet high-pitched songs you sang,
such wisdom you once perceived.

At the closing of the cage,
your heart beating to the anxious rhythm
of a drum.

One day the cage would be your home,
your heart started to beat slowly.

A sad song slowly turned bitter.

Broken

Perceptions fail,
fallen broken pieces of glittering glass
floating over a muddy river.

Nothing is real today,
nothing is real,
only the image itself.

They walk blindly around us,
tripping barefoot on the landscape,
unaware of what they've done.
They expect us to help them see,
when we ourselves can't see.

Off Balance

Through the anger,
we walk in the darkness
looking to fulfill our needs,
slowly falling in,
back to the childhood,
where we once obtained everything we desired.

Submerged in our own expectations of how things
and those around us should be.

They are part of the whole too,
can't be controlled because they have a path of their own.

You can only restrain yourself.

Staggering

The path of life is extensive,
brisk turns at disturbing speeds,
with alcohol in hand along the way.

It is in the beaten path we crash into oblivion,
into a meaningless abyss.

In the alternate path,
one hand soothes you,
while the other grabs the stick.

Eyes Wide Open

I was innocent once too,
remember me?
how I was smiling at the world?
the sun's glistening rays were my sanctuary,
in my thoughts everything was possible.

Too Much

Today it is all about the "yes" or the "no"
I awaken the "maybe,"
giving us time to think about our decisions in life.

We run around like our hair is on fire and
every decision is a life saving one.

Lessons

Whispers in the silence,

longing to be heard,

alive,

that feeling,

books,

bibles,

the mind has long been filled.

Where is the wisdom?

Did you learn?

Precious

The pearls they failed to see.

trapped between all the words,

each one drowning in their own interpretation.

The Game

The elephant and the donkey,
the clock hand turning,
its resonating sound leading to the sound of cuckoo,
their lies tangled in their own egoistic fears.

The elephant and the donkey,
read so many books,
but above all lack compassion
and detachment from good fortune.

The elephant,
crushed the mice it set to war and forgot to apologize.
The donkey,
somehow ran away with our belongings.

The elephant followers,
too impressed with its size.
The donkey followers,
too caught up on the load.

Their followers,

blinding each other with a stick.

The wise ones,

perhaps the working poor who have better things to do.

Disobedience

Smashed against the concrete,
the metallic smell in your blood,
the disappointment in your defeat.

Your victory dance is only a memory,
twirling and twirling,
you let your guard down.

Remember the good days,
remember the good days.

Conflict

Human being,

extraordinarily intelligent,

yet destructive in your own wars.

Stained with the blood of others; revelation or atrocity.

Tainted

Don't be afraid of the spiritual.

fear the human being,

the one who declares wars and betrays.

the sinner.

Don't fear the four legged beasts,

fear the one who only has two,

the one who defiles the world.

Bury
Cupid's Arrow

In the Sand

These lips drowned in the memory of your kisses,
after your departure they became a desolate desert.

Milk and Honey

Velvet siren,

almost saint to the eyes,

who fooled me in a sun bathed reef.

The sweetness of your song

I did hum,

awaiting your return,

next to the jealousy of other men who dreamt of being with you.

Pretentious

I used to give in to it in the mornings,
waking up to the sunlight on my face,
and the idea of new beginnings.

I used to lose control as everything would awaken.
I felt the stiffness,
running to you once more.

The answer,
in my exploring hands.
The pain,
somewhere deep inside me.

I was the visionary,
you were the destroyer,
I got lost in you.

Trail of Love

She must have known,
she must have known,
under her obsession what it really was.

I saw her dark brown eyes and the intriguing smile.
I held my breath,
but was not strong enough,
began to breathe her love.

She touched my lips,
I grabbed her hips,
and I gave way to the warmth in her fingertips.

Everything gently falling apart.

The memories encircling me,
opportunities I had given others..

She must have known.

Beaten Trail

The lust,

drained out of me,

your love,

dried inside you.

Love,

of your heart I never was,

love,

of my heart you could not be.

Too weak,

to withstand this.

You sensed the trail of love,

the ones I left behind.

How free I was,

I did not know,

how much of a prisoner,

I sensed.

No smile was as subtle as yours,
no eyes looked as innocent as yours.

Suicidal love you were to me,
emptiness could not fulfill my hunger for you.

Nothing like this,
no one like you.

Desire to Know

In the beauty of the garden,
this hunger,
this lust,
this passion.

In the garden,
I awoke to your scent,
blown away by the reflection of
the sun on your wet hair.

I entered,
lost myself in you,
a weightless pebble floating at sea.

Until

I committed suicide in the chambers of your heart,
and I swore you felt my pain.

Only then,
were we one.

Under my obsession,
my desire to be with you,
and my inconsolable lust.

Sometimes We Accept Crumbs

I will never be,

your love,

I can only be your lover.

Shine

Slowly and gently like nectar you fall from the empire created in
your mind,
where the sad moments become sweet,
soft in the tender darkness.

But,
even though sad,
even though sad,
walk towards the light,
walk because there is nothing to lose.

Deceive

Wiggling out of my lonely cage,
I found you,
princess of light,
whose eyes blinded my freedom.

Fever

I will hide for you in the solitude,
with no windows,
foreign to sunlight,
drenched in the scent of dried blood.

I will wait for you,
awake,
like the love I have for you.

Feel free to ask for your desires,
this love comes from me.

For you,
it spills into a quick delirium.

Follow

Shadow,
clinging to me.

No hiding place from you, like the sky.

You take my strength and my smile,
leaving no faith.

I will not cry,
for there is nothing here,
the love stopped growing.

Only nostalgia,
what could have been,
or what could never be.

Inclination

Love,
cruel is the feeling with you,
bitterness,
the taste of spoiled meat,
the stench of carcasses.

I tie myself to your feet,
the way a pig is tied up
before neutering.

Then you raise me up,
swinging in my noose,
thinking of the smell of death.

Then,
something inside me gets away,
but you bring it back once more,
tearing it into pieces.

What Is

I searched for you,
longing once again,
the thirst quencher that you once were.

I searched in that same dusty photo,
the one in the beach,
the ocean caressing your feet,
your tanned skin melting onto the sand.

I searched in that photo,
forgetting you were only a mirage stuck in my memory,
a heart print in the blueness of my mind.

Kiss and Betrayal

We fell,
through the rumbling sound of the waves,
the aroma of wet earth,
and the gentle sky.

Don't forget what we felt in our disillusions,
of one who pretends to be another,
like the serpent that pretends to be a friend,
and the apple with its seductive redness.

Back to the Storm

I'll begin to love you once more,

in my head,

as if you were here.

Stupid I was,

I allowed you to let me forget everything,

and I got lost like a love letter,

left in a bottle at sea.

From Summer to Fall

When you awake,
I will be there to soothe your sexual desires.

You will be gone at night,
not a trace of you.
With the sun away,
I'll stay in this cold.

That warmth, the light,
that thing I crave.

Small leaf of autumn,
soon you'll fall just like the others.
Quickly you'll begin to dry and
turn brittle and hard.

From far away I will hear the crunch
when someone steps on you.

Seconds

If in my sadness I find you hidden from me,
even more sad would be to love you all my life.

Too late,
to discover you never loved me.

The Last

This is the last time I will tell my heart I love you.
monster who arrived in a beautiful dawn and
threw my love against the wall,
and seconds later stomped on it until it bled.

Easily, everything becomes night.

Love, love, cruel love.
This is the last time I will tell my heart I love you.

Not Complicated

If you fall in love with a rich woman,

love her,

not her money.

If you fall in love with a promiscuous man

love him,

not his body.

If you fall in love with the same sex,

love their sexual preference,

that's who they are.

Constantly

At times,

I try to refuse the knowledge,

but I know to blind my inner self is to crush love.

For every kiss a love gave me,

the games played with my head.

In one way or another,

I loved savagely but humanely.

Never did I have hate towards the other.

I only felt the pain from the damage.

The last moment,

I will probably feel free,

yet knowing I will be back to finish the rest.

HEALING

Root

Awake with the sorrows of the world,

interconnected,

working as one.

Sad souls,

running against the winds of spirit gods.

An awakening,

a sign of being alive,

dying to be reborn.

Overcome All With Good

Our faces painted,
the despair of dead gods,
we hang onto long fabrics,
hoping to reach for the next one.

Laments of lives forgotten,
upside down crosses,
families mourning,
people struggling to change.

Our hard heads,
the reality in our faces,
the violence we use against
each other,
the things we die for to prove our points.

Bless them and you shall be blessed too.

Wisdom

There are moments….
where the puzzle begins to smell of ashes,
I see the pieces come apart before my eyes,
they turn uncontrollably,
I hear their sound,
my vision is blurry.

I slowly become a shadow,
a torn piece off a map of the world.

I let the emotions defeat me,
hoping my eyes do not open.

The drowning feeling has taken over.
I take a deep breath,
I begin to think about the others…..

High

I once danced on the moon,

when space and time no longer mattered,

letting go of everything,

free from the physical,

when I was only energy.

Star

I haven't created anything,
I am only an instrument like the grail,
someone filled it up from above.

Harmony

In the songs of the birds,
in the rhythm of your heartbeat.

The voice that guides you
and gives you strength.

The sweetest voice of love,
where hate has vanished.

Tribute

Remember when the earth called your name,

with memories of your ancestors,

deep within your bloodstream.

When Things Get You Down

The load,

leading to an aching back.

restless sleep,

confusion of what is day or night.

Don't let it take control!

Pray,

you'll find guidance.

Serenity

They'll try to destroy the peace inside,
shaking you,
the frequency of electroshock therapy,
the slamming of waves against the sand.

Deep inside,
clear springs and warm suns,
nothing crumbles.

Allow

No,

not one more breath,

without you in my heart.

Gently, you drag me into the light.

Life comes deep inside me,

I feel the divine love.

My
Heart
Remembers
Them

Old Maid

Many times the flower looked within,
old maid who failed to show the world the frailty of her soul.

On cold nights,
the tears would roll deep inside her.

Sometimes in the silence of dark days,
infinite number of lovers passed through,
but none,
not one stayed.

In time,
she could no longer reproduce,
her body began to dry.

Many times the flower looked within,
old maid who failed to show the world the frailty of her soul.

Don

Before dawn,
the passionate scent of fresh coffee will no longer awake me.

As I walk through the door in the afternoon,
I will no longer find you resting on the sofa after a long day.

I will no longer hear the shower mid-dream at four in the
morning.

I will no longer hear someone joking about my car never being
clean.
I know you always wanted me to be perfect..

No more bitterness or resentment.
The good in us will heal our wounds.

If ever our relationship struggled it was because you loved me,
and I would avoid you,
because I loved you even more.

Nevermore

Nevermore,

she thought,

nevermore.

Once,

twice,

three times he did the trick.

Nevermore,

she thought,

nevermore.

Once,

twice,

three times he did the trick.

Three times she was condemned and three times betrayed.

Gambling

It was my scent that sent you floating to me,
precious mouse looking for your cheese.

But he,
he was your other half,
I,
I was the half that satisfied you.

Jealousy,
I slightly had for him.

More than anything,
I felt bad for him.
The one who waited and waited,
walking blindly in the heat of summer.

But you,
You were the one I met,
before things got out of control.

I wonder,

I wonder what you're dragging with you,

and what you take home to him.

Naive

Blue bird,

you flew so high,

your tiny brushes of black and white becoming visible

in the sun's resplendence.

Near the peak,

appeared a woman who cut your wings.

Unfortunately,

she tied you to her,

and you allowed her to.

Blue bird,

you flew so high,

with the eyes of others admiring your skill in flight.

Near the peak,

appeared a woman who cut your wings.

As time passed,

your eyes once more found the sunlight.

Without wings and without freedom,

the same you would never be.

Seasoned

They thought peace would arrive once they
handed over their weapons.

The war still lived,
burning painfully deep inside of them,
violently striking their memory,
its deadly scent penetrating their senses.

Their weapons,
stained by the daunting force,
stained by the blood of others.

The screams,
echoing through the dense trees,
and their souls marked by lost dreams.

Rosa Canina

Rose,

soaked under the rain,

hidden in the corner of the world.

Late one night when your love was away,

you invited a man in and made love.

The next day,

your lover did not return.

You knew his son,

so you invited him also.

This one too maintained your inner thirst.

Two generations were not enough,

soon there were more.

Rose,

soaked under the rain,

slowly you began to drown in your desire,

each lover taking a piece of you,

waves slamming over and over against your fragile self.

When your love finally found out,

he also left and did not return.

You remembered once more,

the way your father had abandoned your mother.

Release

In your head,
half dream, half nightmare,
confusion of what is real.

Lost between the dark dreams.

The colorless reality where
the floors and walls become colder,
emotions become stronger.

Those you let down,
disappointed faces,
negative energy.

They were even more disappointed,
when you used the knife to end it all.

Orchard

Once she had bathed in the
feeling of innocence,
showered in dreams.

Then she met him,
the one she gave herself to,
he left a seed growing in her.

The rage would grow too.

You were a star that began to shed the layers,
becoming red.

When the innocence evaporated,
she found a man who loved her,
but she took her anger out on him.

When the flowers she surrounded herself with dried,

he felt the need to leave,

but she held on violently,

and he betrayed her.

You can capture the physical form,

but the heart can never be held captive.

Embryo

The old dream hasn't faded,
still hidden where you once stopped it in its bud.

Another dream came true and you cast it aside.

Again

He began to walk in the dusk of the mind he failed to tame.

Where the physical body became but an instrument
of the truth hidden inside the soul's own defeat.

Where the stone cold body took what it could and shut the rest.

War for Attention

Cute kid,

running with a smile,

latching onto the attention he had been offered.

Soon someone else took his place,

jealousy crept into his heart,

anger webbed onto his face.

He fell in love like silly boys do,

to a young girl who didn't care much.

One day he overheard her tell someone,

"He's ugly, I feel sorry for him."

Soon after,

an older woman stole the twinkle from his eyes.

She made him feel good,

he was hungry and it was all that mattered to him.

Where There Was One

So easily we deceive ourselves,
how puzzling time can be.

When we wait so long for a tyrant to leave,
yet so easily one of the victims will stand up
to possess the role.

Easily,
we forget the pain that longed within us,
melting onto what we hated.

We go to church every Sunday.
Waiting for heaven.
Waiting for heaven.

But if heaven is in our reason,
what is it that we are building for ourselves.

I Will Watch Over You

Memory,
persistent in your purpose.

At moments,
I hear the knife slowly cutting through,
the pain,
the red blood running down my chest,
the numbness kicks in once more.

Tormenting me,
you follow me back to the days I ran laughing
through the trees with the smell of green mangoes
and the later days bitter like karela.

To deny you is to deny myself.

Time sets a stamp on you,
claiming us both as one.

Memory,

persistent in your purpose.

With your destruction,

so is mine.

No name,

no sin.

With my rebirth,

I get lost in your details, aches,

and desires.

You become the sea and I the sun.

Ponder

Ambitions,

innocent,

in the confusion of their own desires.

Dreams,

created under the loneliness of a dark red sky.

Liberating,

the feeling that once made them strong.

Cache

Memory is a message,
a time capsule waiting to be opened.

Years later, lost in the death of its creator.

Ying Yang

Carlos advised Roberto to be more secure of himself.

As always,

Carlos was the happy one,

always the one who gave in to the excitement, the one who

didn't give a damn.

Roberto advised Carlos to be more loving,

that it is better to give kisses instead of bites.

As always,

Roberto was the calm one,

the one who always measured his movements.

"You are I, and I am you," Carlos said.

Brainstorm

I question my awkward behavior,

deep inside the truth,

it holds onto me like a baby pig dangling from its mother's

breast.

A guardian,

she knows something was left behind,

it was meant to be.

Too long,

we torture ourselves with what could have been.

In sadness,

I want to be a kite,

snapped from its string,

flying away on a cool breezy day.

Even then,

I could probably still feel pain.

An orphan,

left alone,

broken dusty portraits,

the sound of broken glass.

Nothing will change inside,

but something wants it to.

I want to meet you,

worthiness,

I may have abandoned you,

with a bad love,

or blocked you from the words

that bitterly cut through my smiling

red sun.

I'll never pretend to be happy.

After death, perhaps I will be a soul,

lingering,

still looking for the answers I was denied.

Paradise Lost

Many times,
I was told not to ask so many questions.
maybe that was my mistake….
always wanting to know more.

Eve,
why did you take the apple?
Adam,
why did you take a bite?
Or was it Evan and Adam?
The message becomes blurry,
too much anger and egoism around me.
Where will we end up?

Is knowledge worth the pain or is it
worse living in ignorance?

Third Eye

I.

Nothing is permanent.

Permanence is something we believed in our youth.

II.

Search within yourself,

the answers are closer than you think,

the journey

is not over,

there is more than this.

III.

Although we may be different,
we must open ourselves up to the life experience,
to the pain and the hurt.
From it,
we cleanse ourselves.

We must look within ourselves,
to find what blinds us,
what makes us uncomfortable.
and to know right from wrong.

The line between right and wrong is so thin at times,
that we must train ourselves to see it clearly.

IV.

Nurture love,

be honest with yourself,

be kind because you are your best friend.

Don't lie to yourself,

be genuine.

You're a ball of energy,

don't let the negative energy in,

release the good energy,

it is continuous.

V.

Pillar of light,

you enter,

all smiles,

king,

your palace damaged,

but never your wisdom.

Holiness,

wise leader.

Ocean of energy,

seer of universal purpose.

33025193R00059

Made in the USA
Charleston, SC
03 September 2014